say a long goodbye

poems on grief

Zach J. Payne

In loving memory,

C.A.W.

1991 - 2009

———

Raid leader, Nimrodel server,

The Lord of the Rings Online.

minstrel extraordinare,

beloved.

Ich bin außer dir.
Ich bin außer dir.
Ich bin außer dir
gar nicht hier.

————

I am beside you.
I am beside you.
I am, except for you,
not even here.

— Wir Sind Helden, *Die Reklamation*

foreword

I've been sitting on this chapbook for a long time.

I'm not sure when I had the idea to put together a collection of poems on grief—it's been at least two or three years, now —but as soon as I started putting it together, something held me back.

I am not what you call a restrained person. If you've seen me post on social media or write blogs over the year, you know that there's very little about my personal life, about my own mental health struggles, that I won't talk about. But something about this collection of poetry felt too raw, too painful, too *much* to put into the world.

My grief has defined a big chunk my life.

As a teen, most of my close friends were people I'd never met before—people I only knew from poetry sites, from online gaming, from roleplaying forums, things like that. They weren't *real*, as so many people liked to tell me.

Shortly after I graduated from high school, one of my closest friends died. I knew her from *Lord of the Rings* roleplay forums, and later from the MMO *The Lord of the Rings Online.*

It's impossible to overstate just how much time we spent together. We talked just about daily. I'd stay late at school, using my computer in the newspaper office so we could talk, in something that approximated real time. She was a big part of my life, a big part of my plans for the future. We were going to go to school together. I was going to study English and theatre, she was going to study history and law.

And then her cancer came back.

Losing her sent my life into a tailspin. I think the worst part of it was that I couldn't tell anybody about it. Not with my new theatre friends, who already thought I was mostly a weirdo, not with my family, who'd dismiss anything to do with "internet people" as not being real.

But I missed her. I grieved her deeply.

It wasn't just her loss, but several others over the years. In childhood, I was pretty well insulated from death. I'd lost a few family members, but death had always been at a distance. In my 20s, I lost so many people—some who were on the periphery of my life, some who were much more central.

I still remember one friend of mine from high school who died, also from cancer. I was struggling at the time, attending a community college where I didn't know anybody. I hadn't made friends, even though I was part of the choir and the newspaper. I was reliant on crappy public transportation, and I hadn't been able to be involved as much as I wanted.

I'd showed up late to our choir performance, a Beatles show-case. I didn't have a lot of goodwill with the professor, and while I stood on stage singing, I felt totally empty, because I realized I didn't know anybody in the crowd. But I looked out, and at the back of the audience, I saw that friend, and it's impossible to describe how much just seeing him grounded me. His presence was an anchor.

And not too long later, he was gone, leaving his spouse and child behind.

Perhaps it sounds selfish, to grieve people so deeply. I know what people would say, that I didn't know them that well, that they couldn't really mean that much to me. But they hit me hard, loss after loss after loss.

And I only had one way to handle it. I put it into words. Those words became an anchor: through the black hole years, and through the long years of healing and failing and hurting and healing and failing all over again.

The words got me through. And maybe they can be a help for you, too.

With love,

Zach J. Payne
March 2022
Hyperbole House
Warren, PA

Miles to Go

i.
these arms are not enough
but I'll carry you as far
as I can—not far enough
from the shifting sand,
the sad shadows that strike
at dusk

jump your bones
and drain you away.

ii.
if I were a superhero
we'd fly
forever and ever on;

but these arms aren't
enough, these bones
are not a battle shield.

I am not enough
to hide you away.

so we run on.

Prayer for a Tired Flower

I hope you grow like roses in soft soil,
be filled with water and sunlight, the purest things.

May you stand against contrary winds, my love;
and your roots sustain you when all else fails.

May you breathe deep in the fresh-breath air
and loving hands prune your death away.

Grow wild and free,
may good luck linger long in your leaves
with all my love.

She is every color of the leaves

she dons a turban as the wheels turn,
gaia exhales, her lungs loose toxic air;
her foliage turns gray and crumbles away.

she changes gears, the cold is yet to come
but she is resolute in enduring the first frost
or so she tries—the centre cannot hold;
i bury her in fallen leaves to feed the new spring.

energy is never lost, she flourishes there,
death begets life, autumn must come
and so she goes. i do not mind the years:
trees will part with leaves, but never with their rings.
she is etched in my hardwood heart.

Dreamer

She dreams in colors. The white of a bride, the gray of old age, pride's whole rainbow. She dreams of color as her colors are leeched out.

Chemotherapy is a bitch that way.

She spends more time sleeping now; her dreams approach infinity. There's a certain beauty in slipping away, like an old flower giving its last bow. Fuck trauma, that's how I want to go.

I hope for her sake that death is a series of dreams, *ad infinitum et ultra*. I don't put much stock in the promise of heaven, but I don't want to believe death is the end of the soul.

I hope for her sake.

Les Filles Mortes

i.
plastic tubes bind
tighter than dungeon irons
around a maiden fair.

astriferous, she soars
beyond cancer's arms
never returning.

ii.
she sleeps
where daisies flourish,
weaving through her hair—

feasting
as meat and bones
become stardust.

The Gift

"But the sons of Men die indeed, and leave the world;

[...] Death is their fate, the gift of Ilúvatar."

-- J.R.R. Tolkien, Quenta Silmarillion

she dreams in crystal
slowly gone to stone, now she
smolders in her endless sleep.

grief crawls like ivy
twisting into hopeful bone.
unconquered: but not for long

for yet she still breathes!
the eucatastrophe waits
without, veiled in bitter tears.

do not pray for death
to rescind its helpful hand,
but call it kindness instead.

Between Realms

You are the colors laced in lightened trees,
the song that echoes wistfully through time,
that substance in the friendly western breeze,
the volta that concludes this lovely rhyme;
my Alpha and Omega, leaving God
to understand: you are my Morning Star,
my Shining Sun, my reason to applaud
the majesty of Earth and Heaven afar.

You are the heart that fights to keep its pace,
though archangels descend to wind their horn,
to leave a pyre, holy fire, in your place
to die, tiny and cold, as you were born.

You were my eyes, my last sight and my first,
the wings that brought me through the very worst.

Intravenous

i. it's a cold day in hell, and i
am running out of steps.

and they sing
gloria, in excelsis deo.

where is God in the ice curtain
that hangs over my ribs
and the stones of this city?

why would i love
this frigid beast that comes
in the cold of night?

ii. the poinsettia wilts,
i can't be bothered
to fetch the watering can.

let it wilt, let it fade,
let it die like she died,
the needle in her arm
draining her rose-light away.

iii. those doctors took my light, too.
don't let these hollow bones fool you.

Those Who Remain

Now point me toward the door to Death's domain,
I need no light; I lost all light with you.
Bedecked in shadows, mourning, I remain
adrift. Restoring you will set life true
or, else, set me to sleep, the slipping stream
will bring me to whatever hither shore
you now call home. Released from waking dreams
I'll take your hand, find peace, just as before.

I would recall you here, whatever cost
be laid against my bones, upon my soul.
The price is unimportant, you were lost
and I would wage the world to see you whole.

I'm scared, though, love; forgive me if I stay
where we are kept apart. I'll come someday.

On the Veneration of St. Valentine, 2010

fiat lux, and there was light ahead
or some illumination, such is
the nature of solitude's fruit, bitter,
bent, weary, a wanderer not knowing
rest or life, just existing another day,
sans raison, sans raison d'être ici.

march through the bloody footprints, son, and trust
this rosy road through hell to go elsewhere.

oh yes, I swallowed the empty words and left
sanity with an iron crucifix, bright
enough to reflect the new moon.

I swallowed the empty words and let
my heart trust the wisdom of St. Peter,
the lie: *caritas numquam excidit.*

astra inclinant, sed non obligant

    as dawn settles to ash, i wonder
    at her, light breaking beyond prisms

    she is crystalline,
    aspect of a girl lost in trade winds
    echoing in plasmic streaks
    in mourning's holy fire.

    i track her in star charts:
    right ascension, declination;
    distance ever increasing.

    she is stellar now,
    etched in heaven's glass

    beyond my terrestrial arms.

The Grave Thereafter

I wonder what becomes of love when Hell
has crowned a lover for His very own;
potential lives be damned, the shadows groan
and steal away the very beat and swell
of life and light and joy, the tinkling bell,
and strip a girl, a child, to blood and bone—
the girl never knowing that she fell.

Or maybe there's a God, what can I say
of spirits dancing, earthly bonds cut free?
Now, world, be cast aright and cast in light
and set her standing there—oh holy day!
alight with life and radiant in glee,
forever spared the darkest strain of night.

To Faerie and On

I love you as the flowers fade to gray,
the stars ascend, the dimming of the day
where other broken lovers turn to pray
I turn from God, to Faery and the fey.

I know you're dancing somewhere in that green
behind closed eyes, inhaling in that scene
before the throne, that ever-lovely Queen,
another ageless soul garbed as a teen.

I miss you even as the hours dance,
though you are dust and shadows at a glance,
abducted by the bitter hands of change.

I miss you now, as days decay to years,
your absence leaving wounds, enforcing fears;
I love you as the days descend to tears.

Ghosts and Ash

We are seventeen again;
I carry an old hymnal
in open palms, tenderness
in voice and touch; we still think
heaven is hearing us, whatever doubts
we have float behind our eyes.

I am missing you, even as we stand
there, appealing to some higher force.
It was all transitory, I told myself so,
and love was a meager thing.
Why live for it--or me, or you, or us,
when life is some jade bird egg
that will crack, no matter how you try
to keep it sacred, keep it safe.

With eyes focused on adamantine gates,
it's easy to burn rope bridges, means
to an end--and God knows you were
a pain in my ass, anyway. Inhale
the old rope smoke like cigarettes--
clockwork muscles release tension--
and maybe this was right. Is this God's sign?

I spend my nights now coughing the past,
memories like phlegm, gumming my chest.
There is no hymnal now, no heavenly gate,
just the dust of three thousand days gone
to ruin, to naught.

Limits

If light can crack across the jagged line,
perhaps our love transcends the bitter void
and I can see the girl that once was mine
in clarity, a softer Polaroid,
without the formal lines that time can etch
into a pretty girl, a sweet auntie,
a grandmother of yore, no voices catch
the dusky rose embroidered on her cheek.

No, she is young, eternal in some glade,
forever dancing, spirits flutter past.
Forever split, an angel and a blade,
that catch the dice, even as they're cast.

For love can cross the line, but we cannot;
affection still intact, but tied in knots.

And We Are Still Bound

If we should walk on planes unknown by
        learned men
perhaps you still exist; our energy is true:
our souls do not decay, and we are not stretched thin,
and we are never split 'twixt life and ether blue.
We linger on in little strings that twitch and pull
and we are bound, a unity of love and light.
No, we are never broken, but a holy whole,
a single organism facing unknown night.

And we may die, indeed, in all the tactile planes
but there are those who hold our fires evermore.
Yes, we are here, untouched by mundane pains;
oh, never live in fear of Heaven's haunting door.

For we are still our songs, yes, even when we die;
our stories are not ended when our lovers cry.

We Dance, Stars as Night Blossoms

Perhaps the two of us belong
at the heart of a collapsing star.

We are heat, manifest:
the light of a thousand dusts
combined into pretty shapes.

We spread into time;
fingers that carry softness,
caress the angry years.

I will fall into you,
over and over and over again;
you, my illumination
and I, yours.

We are the reprise of a song,
gravity bound, tidally locked,
unique in our mathematics.

The fingerprint of two lovers
etched in hydrogen lines,
we dance, eternal orbits
within countless years.

Christ Mass, 2017

it's harder to stay awake
through the ice-water days
when the slurry fills my spine.

i carry my weather with me.
at my core, i am an electric dervish.
rain pools in fingerprint ridges,
wherever i go, i leave those tears behind.

it doesn't make sense to say
"i love you," it wouldn't be wise
to peel the storm windows from
each chamber of my heart, there must be
some piece surviving, one small acorn
and a hand to plant it, one tiny hope
that endures.

there are some things beyond me, survival;
i bind my trust to the textbook grace
of an indifferent god, praying they see
some humanity within me, some song
worth carrying to the next sunrise.

i have stopped asking them
to take the clouds away; there isn't
enough good faith for that. they
do not forgive their crucifixion—
nor will i forgive mine.

but i will remember you, lovers,
beloved, compatriots under wild winds
if i ever come ashore. i thank you.
i return to sleep.

jf

for Jonathan Fierros

i don't know
if the morning's gonna be fine
but we're sure as hell gonna
try
and wake up tomorrow.

the sun will shine
the same as yesterday

everything will look the same
except that little hole becomes
bigger.

and we'll have to breathe
anyway.

The Mourner's Sonnet

If I could roll the clock to sweeter days
would I repent of this, my bitter pain?
Would I walk forward, knowing how this plays,
be swept away in shrouds of icy rain?

For what is pain, in currencies that count
in honeyed gold or minutes flying by?
And where the weregild for my angst and doubt,
for all the years rent empty by my cries?

I have mourned, a million nights and one
and have naught for it! Empty blistered hands
now cast away their mourning -- I am done!
And make my way into the living lands.

But would I cast these years to empty space?
Has grief not left a kind of bitter grace?

for pain is pain

    there is something painful
    in the recollection of i love yous
    said and unsaid,

    an exquisite agony
    that somehow coats my ribs
    in mother-of-pearl; my heart
    in gold.

    the world says that i
    am more beautiful for having loved you
    in the new moon's night,

    but reason says this ache
    is not to be desired.
    i am a goddamn fool
    for ever having loved.

    i wish i could see your face
    in the glowing constellations
    but i survive on smog
    and forgetfulness.

The Price We Pay

after Jay McLean

Our every love is loss; we weigh our hearts
with diamond dust that could transmute to coal
at any given flash. We fall apart,
it wears against the fabric of the soul;
a million little scars, if not a cut,
a coup-de-grâce that renders heaven dead.

Our monkey brains could never fathom what
conspired to our doom. The choice instead,
of opening this misery brings light,
mistakes we carved into our tender skin
unknowing how we'd scar, ugly and tight;
the havoc we would render deep within

by opening our chests: a wink, a smile
becomes a broken heart after a while.

On the Veneration of St. Valentine, 2018

I tell you, love: my heart is lost to stone
and I decay, as water wears away
the fortitude I built, the muscle, bone
and I, exposed, am left to face the day
wherein we celebrate the martyr's heart
forgetting how he died, the rocks, the rods,
the blood that never ceases once it starts
despite how often one invokes the Gods.

Love, would you see me now: your once adored,
or am I just some stranger in his skin;
a monster left to grieve, alone, abhorred,
unable to restore the boy he'd been?

And do not say it: time will ease the ache
for time has come and gone, and still, I break.

Somehow There's Still Sunlight

i.

The dreams come to me in the soft-frost hours before
sunrise. Even as heat rises through my comforter cocoon, my
bones freeze from the marrow out. These bones are unlovely;
I am no beautiful thing, so broken by the phantoms that rise
from Tartarus to wind through my ribcage, to make me
cough and cry and ache.

Today is day 1193. God help me.

I know that I am supposed to sleep and rest and rise and
shine; my life has been overtaken by the middle way, 100
million odd seconds of haze, arrayed in long procession. Oh,
my dear, I have taken the long, low road through Hell, where
the rocks breathe strange shadows, the rising miasma barely
strong enough to cut through the blurred curtain of my tears.

That, love, is the story since you've been gone. I do not
begrudge your eager sleep; those hours dragged on, fire and
ice plugged into your skin, living on promises that died like
stone-grown flowers.

I do not begrudge your eager sleep. I only wonder when my
eyes will dry. When will I be able to see the world without
your light?

ii.

They do not tell you that the world walks away. Yes, they

understand pain, until the pain lingers like whatever asshole pianist broke the sostenuto and let this grief echo long after the music died.

Oh, they have loves and they have lives and, after a while, they throw out the dead flowers. But you, I still tend, someone must tend you, I cannot throw you out. I have managed to weather the winter by a thorn's breadth. I manage to keep on, living some silent stasis, excruciated but alive.

iii.

Perhaps you don't see the sunflowers that grow in the dark corners of my mind, but I promise you, they are there. Dawn is not instantaneous, indeed, she marches in slow regiment with heavy steps, cracking slow, tentative, on the far horizon.

I fail, in most moments and on most days. My heart pumps in retrograde and my eyes look ever backward to brighter days, seeking the rosiest light.

I have worshipped your memory with a simple stupidity, failing to see the complexities inherit in a beating heart and an electric mind. I have torn you down to my eyeline and made you about me. I have been the center of my own constellation, orbiting too long among icy worlds of concrete grief, to the exclusion of brighter worlds, far away.

I confess my failures, but amends are harder. Be patient with me; allow the jagged cracks of light to break through me. I am not perfect. I am not selfless, or even good most of the time. But I remember my better self, reflected in the sky of your eyes. And that is the gospel of my grief: my story was better with you in it.

But the story goes on, and so must I.

Articles of Faith: On Grieving

We taught you how to sleep. The darkness drapes
around our tired bones. A soothing sleep
now sings to us, and every muscle scrapes
its final surge of strength. We dig in deep
and give our all at last. It's not so sad
when pain departs and freedom finally rings
with effervescent grief. We feel so mad,
but peace has come. The spirit truly sings
beyond the walls of all the woes we hold.
It's over now. And though we shed our tears,
we are forever found. We are not cold.
We aren't always subject to our fears.

So cry away, but cling ever to hope.
Our weary eyes can't see from Heaven's scope.

& encore

If love's a knot that holds us fast,
are we then tethered to the past?
If every kiss, an iron bond
attaches us to those beyond
the circles of this fragile life—
how keen the blade of Memory's knife!

It cannot break what love has bound
nor can it take the joy I've found
in loving you, in every day,
remembering you in every way.

If love's a knot that binds us so,
then so be it, for love will grow
beyond the reach of time and space,
eternity recalls your grace.

It Isn't Easy Going On

after Krystal Sutherland

The universe absolves the grief we hold
as leaden anchors tightly to our chests.
In tiny currents, atoms, ever bold,
will grind the stones we've sown into our vests
and let us float away. Forgiveness comes
to lift the heavy judgment from our heads,
undeeming dooms we spoke with lips so numb;
a *mal de coeur* that would not see us dead
but shattered. "This is justice, don't you know?"
The voice within insists, and we receive
the sentence handed down–and so we go,
not knowing that the little voice deceives.

A year is not forever, nor a day;
through herculean grace we're made okay.

the song of the end

we say goodbye again, into the mist,
a simple wave, a hug, and then the part
and every love we love shall stand dismissed--
a bitter pill. although it is a start
that brings some new great wonder, it's an end
beyond all ends, a line chipped into stone
and all those things whereon our hearts depend
are cut away -- and we stand stark alone.

we will rebuild, reflourish, something new
will grow inside the absence, some new song
shall rise in time, some harmony ring true--
but something good must die. We go along.

even with the good, grief will insist:
for memories, damned memories, persist.

On the Veneration of St. Valentine, 2022

My love, I've lost the pretty little song
you used to sing so sweetly to the stars.
I carried it so far, brought it along
a piece of you that I could keep in jars,
unperishing, the years will melt away
the finer points of memory. I weep
for everything we lost, the brighter days
we never got to see. Perhaps we'll keep
the love we bore in life, but I think not.
The years are not so merciful, you know.
And every little firefly I've caught
will die eventually, they have to go.

But even knowing that, I will not part,
not willingly, with you. It hurts my heart.

———

Originally published in "The Daily Cuppa",

Katie Michaelson, ed.

Benediction for the Lost

for Bailey Holt and Preston Cope

I want to believe
that Thanatos is a mother, she wears
a robe of sweet starlight, swaddling clothes
for wayward children returning.

May her shoulder be
large enough to carry their tears
and burdens. Mother, soothe them
as their electric wonder fades.

When Sapience fails, humanity
standing forsworn, unreliable
at every turn, let serenity be
mother's aegis.

Let peace befall them
as they return to the stellar forge.

May the universe remake them
under a kinder star
far from here.

a letter to a girl past the rainbow bridge, who fought her great war.

Dear you, my sister in arms, while you still carried them in this tenuous sphere, I wish you the greatest peace. I know what it means to be weighed down by the holographic voices, to seek the mystic serenity of the longest sleep. I pray that you stand under a beautiful sky, wherever you are.

I hope there is no war in that sacred city, no guilt or remorse or pain or angst. You have held those monsters on your shoulder blades for far too long. Time has a way of dilating, where even a second can feel like an eternity; relative frames demand a reconsideration of time's skin and bearing.

I know the weight of those concrete shoes, and what it means to untie them. You were here for as long as your feet could keep you up, even if that eternity was a butterfly's breath by some other angle. You deserve to breathe at your own pace, without Atlas's burden held against you. I hope you have found that grace.

I, too, bear that weight. Someday, I will seek the same footpath that you found, depositing my bones on this weary road and seeking some far-off light. I have tried to slip my skin before, and will again, unless some happenstance claims me first, or else some trick of fate. This is how our bodies were built, the chemicals within twisting the world that presses against our eyes. But I still take my steps, with the peace of knowing that what will be will be.

There will always be tears in this world. We are built to shed them without shame; only the "wisdom" of thinkers past have bound the baggage to them. We will weep those tears. We will cause them. That is the way of the globe beneath our feet. There are no walls thick enough to keep human nature at bay.

I know that you know the fabric you cut, the oceans of heavy air that your choice poured into the hearts around you; one monster among the legion that fought for your gaze. I know that you loved as best you could love. Then came the moment where you had to love yourself more, in whatever way you could.

I hope that Thanatos and whatever Holy Ghosts there are, whatever psychopomps there be, can take our jigsaw hearts and make something whole out of them. We do not deserve to be broken throughout all of space and time.

For now, we down here hold ourselves together with prayers and swears and the strongest duct tape we can find. Bear our worries no mind. We will see you soon.

With love,

your brother beneath the stars.

& i feign piety before the ultraviolet apocalypse

after jennifer niven

i pass another marble jesus
& then i step into a room that glows.

gabriel and jesus are raising the dead,
hands reach upward, across
the ceiling like stars.

ask the angels
to bring loved ones back;
give them a happy eternity.

in the outstretched palm of jesus,
i see it -- the one thing
& so i pick it up, the offering
i've brought -- a butterfly ring.

i stay awhile longer and then go
blinking into daylight. two sets
of stairs, side by side, and a sign:

DO NOT WALK ON THE HOLY STAIRS
ASCEND ON YOUR KNEES

i count 28 steps.
i drop to my knees and go up.

An Echo in Shattered Glass

Perhaps you are the memory of joy
bespoken of my bones, some lighter day
when I, so veiled in light, a lovely boy
could while away the hours, truly play
with memories like dreams, but meant to be,
imagining a future drawn in stone,
a certainty that I could taste and see
when I was neither lost nor left alone
to wallow in my grief, the lakes of loss
that overwhelm and leave me treading air
and breaking promises I'd never cross
back when I was young and life was fair.

Perhaps you were my hope—or just a dream,
an echo left to temper hopeless screams.

To Wake Again

If I should learn to love when hope is lost,
and wander, weary, back to living life,
I wonder, truly, what will be the cost
of spending all these years upon a knife
that cuts both ways, my body and my friends
have felt its stinging kiss, have run away,
betrayed by means that never found their ends.

And now the sleeper rises to the day
that broke and crested with no need of him
now, I have no idea where to start
this broken heart, these desiccated limbs;
this actor has no notion of his part.

But what are parts? The mere pretense of joy
is not enough to fix a broken boy.

For Violet and Cody, Who Remain

after Jennifer Niven and Gayle Forman

i.
I will not elegize her,
the words will not come, and, anyway,
I prefer not to close the pages,
to bind the book; it is not finished,
we are not finished; she is not done.

I cannot clip those wings.

ii.
I will take to this great perhaps
and cling to the memories, jewels
in the firmament that threatens
to swallow all; these threads
are not enough, are everything I have.

I must tape myself together
and face the question:
why?

iii.
Can we speak to the years ahead,
to the dreams that flit between Faerie and Hell?
I would have you back; I would give—
but no. This is done, this is sealed,
you are gone.

I am not fond of finality,
but this is our end.

I never hoped for heaven
until I loved and lost you.

To the Torchbearers from the Dearly Departed

for Lori and Wayne Earl

We live on, not in Heaven, but in love,
kinetic love, in motion still we stand
in all dimensions, not merely *above*.
We linger on in fingerprints and hands
that interact, by chance, with you. We know
and stand as sentinels 'twixt here and gone.
Blow out your vigil light, our bones below
are not for you to weep and gnaw upon.

Your tears are not forbidden, but the rain
that washes out your life must dry away
for if your soul should yield to storm and pain
our dreams become as dust. Make better days.

Yes, we surpass our corpses, do not fear;
in everything you do, we're standing near.

& we were good kids, who'd do everything different next time

i.

We painted angels in the sand, tracing concentric halos guilty of shining too bright, we little hypocrites devoid of Heaven's functional wavelength. We loved ourselves, left St. Peter grumbling as he drew double daggers next to our names in the Book of Life.

We were quiet kids, pretending to mind mother's manners, miming rebellion in inner monologues, pretending at freedom while the other kids just didn't give a shit.

We were lunar liars, serenading and seducing ourselves under the saints's twinkling eyes, allergic to movie popcorn and the freshness of Friday nights. We drank our concentrated tears in shotglasses, calling it vodka just because our throats tasted fire.

We dedicated our lives to headphones and ASCII, clinging to the delusions of superiority that kept us growing. One day, someday, someday soon, we would have our crowns and heavenly treasure, eternal life worth living. We would be so much better than all these sinful fucks.

And thus we lived: afraid of Sin, dying slow suicides in the name of being good.

ii.

If I could unbury her, strip away the scars that cancer left in

capillaries and bone, I would tell her to live. I would hoist
her to the highest star, tell her to inhale the ionizing radia-
tion. We're all gonna die anyway, and she actually did.

We didn't have to drive ourselves into the rocks, or stand at
altar call and declare a jihad against our human nature. We
were created, not in the cruel granite of Adam's God, but in
some softer stone, spun of marble and stardust, so much
sweeter.

This was always the Doom upon our skins, a sentence
pronounced against our bones even before we could crack a
Bible open and align our bodies against its contrary winds.

We were always going to die.
We would have been just fine.

She is a Paradox, Somewhere High Above

I beheld you as sunlight,
the sum of colors, bound in warmth
traveling in straight progression.

Once here,
now gone.
Always lingering.

You are a particle and a wave,
contradictions that slip,
water through my fingers

my mind a sieve
but heart untouched.

You were what you were
and are what you are;
astriferous now, unblemished;
your face plain
in the black crystal firmament.

Still here,
always here.

Stella

Perhaps you know that love can carry on
through grief and solid stone, against the stars
that burn in opposition. When we're gone
it will endure: and life will never mar
the garden we have tended deep within,
the roses we have borne in hope and grief,
the blemishes that come with petty sins,
the stellar forges made of our belief.

Perhaps you know that I will love you hence,
though maybe I, in time, shall close my wounds
for I am not so mighty. Grief relents;
like waves, it ebbs away, but ne'er concludes.

So, too, with love: infinity and more,
the feelings we release persist, endure.

A Girl, A Ghost

Still dusted in day-old makeup and
half-baked from stage lights,
the actor faces Yuletide ghosts
in the shrink's office.

Cold-infused with sunlight
and populated with veterans
in the guise of disheveled children
reeling, so amazed at being alive
they can ignore the downward tug
of mother's lips.

They haunt him, yes,
but horror and hope arrive
haloed in light, Marley minus chains,
chemical romance leaking from her ears.

He knows well the hymn
and better this face, familiarity
catches spark and burns
behind his eyes.

She settles into molded plastic,
sunflower earrings belie the burden
that she, Atlas, carries on her shoulder
and around the eyes that've only seen
fifteen years or so.

Flashes of blue and

a dirty blonde cascade
remind him of a girl,
her martyrdom earned in cancer's wars;

even in subtle hints,
he draws facial trigonometry between
present and past.

A hung jury behind a hanging mouth,
he bites his tongue on the name
of a girl seven years dead
as she greets her therapist
and walks back somewhere.

anniversary

for a.s.k.

i miss you as you ascend at right angles
into some imaginary plane, each photon
that once kissed your skin loosens,
lighter from my eyes, beyond,
beyond

(and i know, or,
at the very least, suspect
that someday you will
disappear for good.)

there are enough echoes
of you still that i might
try
to tie them all back
into a flesh and blood girl,
smiling,

ghost over ghost, bound,
until you are corporeal
again

each memory is a jewel
in its own right, and you
were the sparkle running through
tying them together

still something, even as
you stretch into
some uncountable infinity
beyond my fingertips.

A Thin Line Called Optimism

Another year: come kindly, I am weak
and weary of the days that, merciless
have broken these old bones. I'd rather seek
an optimistic song–is it worthless?--
I couldn't say. But still I raise my voice,
defiant to the end–is this the end?--
It's no beginning. If we have the choice
let us go singing. Grief will have to bend
to hope, a tiny jewel in firmament
much darker than the skies that press us in.
Look how it shines! This star is permanent.
Aye, even when the clouds come rolling in.

I try to smile. Oh, heavens, how it aches.
This year: be magic, let the sorrows break.

In Loving Memory, J.S.E.

I saw you in the stars, these hieroglyphs
have learned your name, your face, by perfect heart
and I can only marvel from these cliffs,
this little speck of dirt. We are apart.

Through all these miles still, you shine the same
but amplified, for now you are unbound
and undiminished by all earthly pain--
Now in your stellar light this heart is found,
is once again recalled to kindred hearts,
the home by which we kindle our own light.
Although you are recalled at Heaven's start,
we keep you here with us, vibrant and bright.

Although you shine still strong we miss you here,
your voice, your laugh, your love: we miss you dearly.

On a Dove, Taking to the Sky

for Naya Rivera

The Lord in Heaven teaches us to dream
and, someday, we return unto that host;
all metaphors belie that spirit-stream
beyond our comprehension. At the most
we see a jagged light, a rainbow cast
in ultraviolet, well beyond all sense;
a promise of the kingdom that will last
despite the heat death destined to commence.

Now you will never need these bones again,
no matter shall pin down your vital force.
We bid you go and rest with saintly kin
without egregious grief or long remorse
for we are temporary in these shapes;
forever only lives in our escapes.

For CAW, After Nine Years

I wonder if you've grown past how you died
into some wholesome youth, past pain and flesh,
your skin ablush with color long denied,
your bones untouched by death, body refreshed
beyond all hope, for you are sunk in stone,
pallor unchanging 'til the world should end
but I cannot imagine you alone
diminished and decaying, love defends
against such mortal woes. You're young and soft,
awash with light, with stardust in your breath—
now I will hold you, graven girl, aloft
and with my life prevent your second death.

Yes, I will grow you where the world did not,
sustain you through the battles left unfought.

Not Quite Ten Years Later

Exhale her ghost and watch her spirit rise
to some High Heaven nestled in the stars.
Imagine not this grace as her demise,
but freedom! You have rent the iron bars
that drain your inner flame relentlessly
and set a frigid lock upon your chest.
She will remain. Look skyward and you'll see
her secret sign. She is at her best
and free to wander back if Fate bestows
another temple for her vital light.
If not, we'll meet wherever spirits go
and Death shall lose the horror of its bite.

Though time will not pass lightly, it will wear
like water on a boulder. I'll be there.

On the Veneration of St. Valentine, 2020

Does love, like radiation, seep away
into some smaller substance? Give a year
or ten or fifty million, half a day,
and half our love has boiled off, the tears
less toxic now. In time, can I reclaim
the meltdown in my chest? Will forests grow
despite all the destruction and the flames
that cleared me out? I don't suppose we'll know
within this lifetime or even the next
if it is safe, cut down the hazard tape
that binds these ribs; obscure the dire text
on every signpost here, let love escape
into the wider world. This tainted heart
after its long sequestering, would start.

how to tell if your body is real

after a.s.k.

I can feel my bones. I have bones, I think;
it seems my skin is slipping, slack and pooling.

And what are muscles? Atrophy sets in;
I diminish, dust and empty clothes
carried on electric cool currents,
strewn across this living room.

Living? Yes. Dammit, I'm alive.
A dustpan, please. If I can't be whole,
then give me the dignity of being in one place;
self contained, sweep me into grandmother's urn.

She's not here, but I am, I am.
I need the help. I'm still here --

if only by a flutter. Yes,
that's the heart flying, myocardium intact
when everything else is gone.

Sweep me together and, heart beating,
I will rise from dust.

He Breaks the Soil but Never Breaks His Heart

I tended you, a flower in my heart;
your roots delved deep and I could never mind
the loss of blood. I loved to see you grow.
We were enough; I was content to go
through spring and spring again. We had no snow.
I tended you, a flower in my heart.
And all was good, a minute or a month,
we never had enough. We were entwined.

But winters come and go. And love can die;
neglect or circumstance, it ends the same.
I tended you, a flower in my heart,
and we were left with misery and blame
for many painful years. But on we grow
and scars will form if left for long enough.
There's no regret, not now or evermore:
I tended you, a flower in my heart.

———

Originally published in "The Daily Cuppa",

Katie Michaelson, ed.

The Confluence of Stars

after Jennifer Niven

I never understood how planets pull
beloved to beloved, tiny strings
encompassing our everything, the whole
of us, even the mysteries, the things
we'd rather laugh away. A smile, a wink,
and nobody unravels the disguise
or so I prayed. I never dared to think
that you would pull me into open skies
and strip me down, unveiling all the grief
I wrote unto myself, a second skin;
enamor me in loveliness, belief
that something beautiful could dare begin
where sorrow grows; a tender beating heart
could flourish after being torn apart.

How It Starts

after Bree Lowdermilk

i.
this is how it starts:
i am slow to waking, it
has been a long time since something
pierced the great sleep that veils me,
a phantasm of the old sunlight
back in my jeunesse, that thorned crown;

oh, how could i know
the sweetness of small indignities
compared to the death knell to follow?

i, faced with the black hole
retreated to the mesmer's realm,
in so saving some small part of myself
in trust for better days.

ii.
will you recall me? will yours be
the voice that cuts, precise through
the echo of faerie i have set around my bones?

i am girt with no small magic; i have thrown
every spell i know into protecting myself
worthless though i be, i am
my most prized possession. this is it.
this is all i have.

iii.
do not wake me
until the world should change. is pi
some solid number? does gravity draw
away from mass? will i be able to repair
the mortal wounds inflicted in days past?

or, else, will you love me
with all my flaws intact?

i will wake if you call me, i will set aside
my cares and claims, demand no weregild

for the years of my lost youth. i will rise,
if you will have me among the living,
unchecked, unbound by the fetters
that kept me oh so small and sad.

And I'm not sure that I'm okay,
but I get stronger every day.
And when I'm scared I won't get through,
I know I'll find the good things, too.
I know I'll find the good things.
I know I'm finding good things.

— Preston Max Allen,
"Finale", *We Are The Tigers*

acknowledgments

It isn't easy to stand by someone who's deep in grief. I'm grateful for everyone who loved me through the bad days, everybody who celebrated with me on the good days and sustained me through the bad ones, to everyone who was, in the words of my dear friend Jennifer Niven, "a bright place". You know who you are.

To all of the people who loved me, and who had to pull away to protect your own mental health. I understand, and I love you.

about the author

Zach J. Payne is, to borrow the words of Lin-Manuel Miranda, "a polymath, a pain in the ass, a massive Payne." He is a poet and novelist, and part of the staff at Ninja Writers. He can usually be found belting show tunes, if the LMM quote didn't make that obvious.

Originally from Southern California, Zach currently lives in Warren, Pennsylvania. After several years, still doesn't like the winters.

http://zachjpayne.com
http://estelrandir.substack.com

facebook.com/zjpwrites

twitter.com/zachjpayne

instagram.com/zachjpayne

tiktok.com/@zachjospayne

goodreads.com/zachjpayne

www.ingramcontent.com/pod-product-compliance
Lightning Source LLC
Chambersburg PA
CBHW051348150726
48000CB00003B/1099